K GRADE

Foundational Skills
Workbook

SAVVAS
LEARNING COMPANY

Savvas Learning Company LLC, 15 East Midland Avenue, Paramus, NJ 07652

Savvas™ and **Savvas Learning Company**™ are the exclusive trademarks of Savvas Learning Company LLC in the U.S. and other countries.

Savvas Learning Company publishes through its famous imprints **Prentice Hall**® and **Scott Foresman**® which are exclusive registered trademarks owned by Savvas Learning Company LLC in the U.S. and/or other countries.

ReadyGEN® and **Savvas Realize**™ are exclusive trademarks of Savvas Learning Company LLC in the U.S. and/or other countries.

Unless otherwise indicated herein, any third party trademarks that may appear in this work are the property of their respective owners, and any references to third party trademarks, logos, or other trade dress are for demonstrative or descriptive purposes only. Such references are not intended to imply any sponsorship, endorsement, authorization, or promotion of Savvas Learning Company products by the owners of such marks, or any relationship between the owner and Savvas Learning Company LLC or its authors, licensees, or distributors.

ISBN-13: 978-0-328-96297-6
ISBN-10:   0-328-96297-X
10 2021

Contents

Decodable Stories

Phonics

High-Frequency Words

I am bear.

4

Decodable Story *I Am!*
Letter Recognition *Aa, Bb, Cc, Dd, Ee*

I Am!

I am ant.

1

 I am dog.

2

 I am cat.

3

Am I iguana?

Am I monkey?

Am I kangaroo?

Decodable Story *Am I?*
Letter Recognition *Ff, Gg, Hh, Ii, Jj, Kk, Ll, Mm, Nn*

Name _____

Am I?

I am fish.

I am goose.

I am horse.

I am the little rabbit.

Am I the little seal?

4

Decodable Story *Little Me!*
Letter Recognition *Oo, Pp, Qq, Rr, Ss*

Little Me!

Am I the little otter?

I am the little otter.

Am I the little pig?

I am the little pig.

2

Am I the little quail?

I am the little quail.

3

Am I the little zebra?

4

Decodable Story *Am I Little?*
Letter Recognition *Tt, Uu, Vv, Ww, Xx, Yy, Zz*

Name _____

Am I Little?

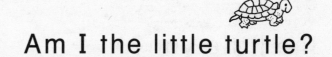

Am I the little turtle?

I

7

Am I the little van?

2

Am I the little

watermelon?

3

I walk to a little school.

4

Decodable Story *Little Mouse*
Target Skill /m/ Spelled *Mm*

Little Mouse

I am a little mouse.

I

I walk to a little school.

I am a little moose.

I walk to a table.

Decodable Story *Tam!*
Target Skill /t/ Spelled *Tt*

Tam!

I am Tam.

I am a turtle.

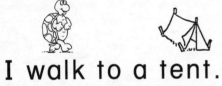

I walk to a tent.

I walk to a turkey.

I have gum.

I have gum.

Decodable Story *I Have!*
Target Skill /a/ Spelled *Aa*

I Have!

I have a cat.

The cat is little.

I have a rat.

The rat is little.

I have a ham.

The ham is little.

2

3

I have the sock.

4

Decodable Story *Sock Sack*
Target Skills /s/ Spelled *Ss*

Sock Sack

I have a sack.

I

 The sock sack is little.

 The sock is little.

2

3

I like to pat Pam.

4

Name _____

Pat the Cat

I like to pat my cat.

I

I pat my cat, Pam.

We pat Pam.

2

3

We like the caps.

4

Decodable Story *The Cap*
Target Skill /k/ Spelled *Cc*

The Cap

I have a cap.

I

19

The cap is my cap.

I like my cap.

He is a little pig.

4

Decodable Story *Tim the Pig*
Target Skill /i/ Spelled *Ii*

Name _____

Tim the Pig

Tim the pig is little.

I

Tim the pig can tap it.

2

Tim the pig can pat it.

3

Sit, pat, sip.

Name _____

Sam, Sit!

Sam, sit.

4

Decodable Story *Sam, Sit!*
Target Skill /i/ Spelled *Ii*

I

Sam, pat.

Sam, sip.

Nat sat.

Nan sat with Nat.

4

Decodable Story *Nan and Nat*
Target Skill /n/ Spelled *Nn*

Nan and Nat

I am Nan.

I am Nat.

We have nets.

1

Nan is with Nat.

Nat can nab with a net.

Nat nabs with the net.

Nan nabs with the net.

Rin ran to Rip.

Rip ran.

4

Rin the Rat

Rin is a rat.

She is a little rat.

I

Rin likes to tap.

She can tap.

Rip ran to Rin.

He is with Rin.

Pit ran to the dish.

Pit did.

4

Decodable Story *Pit Did!*
Target Skill /d/ Spelled *Dd*

Pit Did!

Pit can see the duck.

Pit ran with the duck.

Pit did.

1

Pit can see the doll.

Pit ran to the doll.

2

Pit can look at the door.

Pit ran to the door.

Pit did.

3

I see a fin for me.

Look at the fin.

Decodable Story *For Me!*
Target Skill /f/ Spelled *Ff*

For Me!

I see a fan for me.

Look at the fan.

I see a fox for me.

Look at the little fox.

2

I see a fish for me.

Look at the little fish.

3

Little Rob is not sad.

Little Rob can have
the top.

Little Rob is sad.

He is little.

4

Little Rob

Decodable Story *Little Rob*
Target Skill /o/ Spelled *Oo*

I

Little Rob is on a mat.

He is sad.

Little Rob can see a top.

Can he have the top?

It is not on the rat.

It is in the pot.

4

Decodable Story *A Cap for Tom*
Target Skill /o/ Spelled *Oo*

A Cap for Tom

Tom can have a cap.

Is the cap on Tom?

I

The cap is not on Tom.
See the cap.

The cap is not on Tom.
It is on the rat.

I like my hat.

Do you like my hat?

4

Decodable Story *I Have!*
Target Skill /h/ Spelled *Hh*

I Have!

I have a hat.

The hat is little.

That is my hat.

I

The hat is on me.

It is my little hat.

Do you have a little hat?

I can hop with the hat.

I can hit with the hat.

2

3

Lad can hop on the lid.

I can do that.

Are we on the lid?

4

Decodable Story *Lad and Me*
Target Skill /l/ Spelled *Ll*

Lad and Me

Lad is my cat.

Lad is little.

Do you like Lad?

1

I like Lad.

Lad can sit in my lap.

Lad can sit a lot.

2

Lad can hop.

Lad can hop a lot.

I can do that.

3

I can tap.

Tap is like trap.

Do you see one trap?

4

Decodable Story *My Words*
Target Skill Consonant Blends

Name _____

My Words

I have one cap.

Cap is like clap.

Can you clap?

I

41

I see one cab.

Cab is like crab.

Can you see three?

2

I can see one pot.

Pot is like spot.

Do you see two?

3

Can you see four frogs?

Lin and Hap can see
five frogs.

4

Decodable Story *How Many?*
Target Skill /g/ Spelled *Gg*

Name _____

How Many?

Lin and Hap can see
one dog.

I

43

Lin and Hap can see
two kids.

Lin and Hap can see
three pigs.

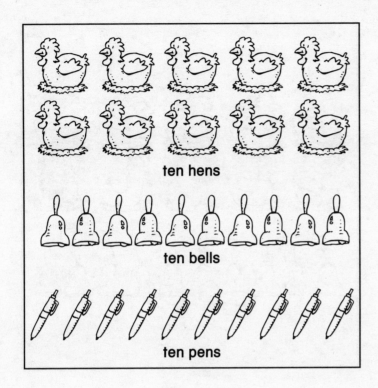

ten hens

ten bells

ten pens

I see ten, ten, ten!

4

Decodable Story *Ten, Ten, Ten!*
Target Skill /e/ Spelled *Ee*

Ten, Ten, Ten!

I have a pet hen.

Do you see my hen?

I can see ten.

I

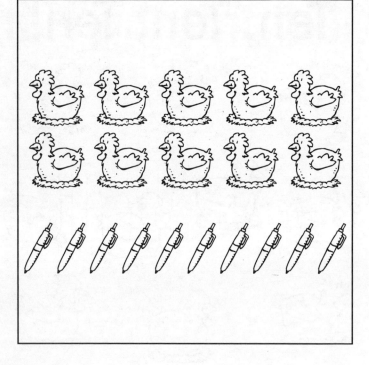

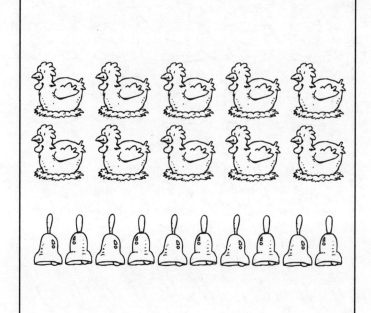

I have a fat pen.

Do you see my pen?

I can see ten.

2

I have a red bell.

Do you see my bell?

I can see ten.

You can see the tent.

You can see the nest.

I have a pet.

Decodable Story *Ted and the Pet*
Target Skill /e/ Spelled *Ee*

Ted and the Pet

I am Ted.

I have a pet.

My pet is big.

I met my pet here.

My pet is in the tent.

It is a big tent.

My pet can go to the tent.

My pet has a nest in the tent.

It is a big nest.

You can get on the big, blue jet.

You can go with Jen and Will.

4

Decodable Story *Jen and Will*
Target Skill /j/ Spelled *Jj*, /w/ Spelled *Ww*

Name _____

Jen and Will

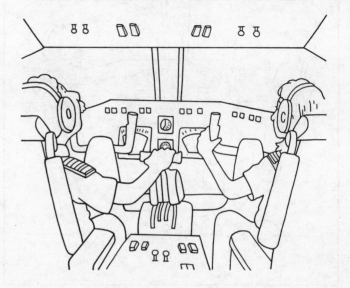

Jen and Will get on the jet.

It is a big, blue jet.

I

Jen and Will have jobs
on the jet.

Jen and Will like the jobs.

2

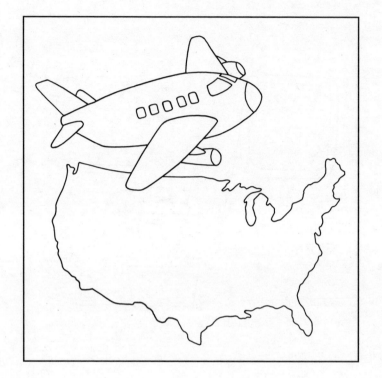

Jen and Will get the jet
to go.

They can see you.

3

Max can see his pal Rex.

Max and Rex can mix
yellow and red.

Decodable Story *Max*
Target Skill /ks/ Spelled *Xx*

Name _____

Max

Max is six.

He hid in a box.

He hid from his mom.

Max can look like a fox.

He has four legs.

2

Max can mix blue and green.

It is an ox.

3

Jud ran to his pals.

Jud said, "Let us go in!

We will have fun!"

4

Decodable Story *Fun for Jud*
Target Skill /u/ Spelled *Uu*

Fun for Jud

The sun was hot.

Jud got up from bed.

I

Jud has to have a plan.

What can he do for fun?

Jud will see his pals.

What will they do for fun?

Jan and Gus are on the rug.

Jan and Gus are pals.

4

Decodable Story *Jan and Gus*
Target Skill /u/ Spelled *Uu*

Jan and Gus

Jan and Gus are pals.

They like to have fun.

1

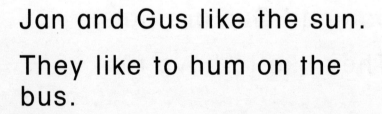

Jan and Gus like the sun.

They like to hum on the bus.

2

Jan and Gus see a bug.

They run in the mud.

3

He will zap the tag.

Val has got the red top.

Copyright © Savvas Learning Company LLC. All Rights Reserved.

Val's Top

Val and Mom come in a van.

They will go to look for a top.

Val and Mom see a top.

They can zip it up.

The top is red.

Val and Mom like the top.

Tim ran to the end.

Tim had a rest.

4

Decodable Story *Run, Tim*
Target Skill /y/ Spelled *Yy*, /kw/ Spelled *Qq*

Run, Tim

Tim ran past his sis.

She said,

"You can not quit yet."

1

Tim ran up a hill.

His dad said,

"You can not quit yet."

2

Tim ran and ran.

His mom said,

"You can not quit yet."

3

Vin will zip the bag.

He and the bag will go on a trip.

4

Decodable Story *Vin and the Bag*
Target Skill Review

Vin and the Bag

Vin had a bag.

The bag is a big bag.

I

61

He got one big can.

He got one little net.

He got one little kit.

He got one big rag.

Dad will spin the top.

Dad can spin it.

Dad can get the top
to spin.

4

Spin the Top

Bob got a top.

Bob will spin the top.

I

The top will not spin.

The top will not go.

2

Help! Help!

Help me spin the top.

It will not spin.

Help! Help!

3

The hen had little ones.

Jim and Kim have lots of little hens.

4

Decodable Story *Jim and Kim*
Target Skill Review

Jim and Kim

Jim and Kim had a pet.

They had a pet hen.

The hen was in a pen.

I

Jim had fun with the pet hen.

Jim fed the hen.

Kim had fun with the pet hen.

Kim got a nest for the hen.

2

3

Gus grabs the bug.

Gus lets the bug go.

4

Decodable Story *Gus and the Bug*
Target Skill Review

Gus and the Bug

Gus will hug his mom.

Gus gets on the bus.

I

Gus sat with his pal Wes.

The sun was hot.

A bug got on the bus.

It sat with Gus and Wes.

2

3

Sam is a cat.

Sam will sit in a lap.

He will nap.

Decodable Story *What Pets Do*
Target Skill Review

What Pets Do

Peg is a dog.

She will tug.

She will dig.

Hal is a pet pig.

He will run in his pen.

He will go in the mud.

2

Tad is a pet frog.

He will hop.

He will swim.

3

I am Jen.

I can hang from my legs.

What can you do?

4

Decodable Story *What Can You Do?*
Target Skill Review

What Can You Do?

Here is Ned.

Ned can run fast.

Ned can run and run.

I

Look at Ken.

He fed the big dog.

He fed the little dogs.

See Kim jump.

She can go from me to you.

She can jump from here
to here.

Name _____

 **Write**  **Color**

_____
- - - - - - - - - - - - - - - - -
_____

_____
- - - - - - - - - - - - - - - - -
_____

Mm

_____
- - - - - - - - - - - - - - - - -
_____

_____
- - - - - - - - - - - - - - - - -
_____

_____
- - - - - - - - - - - - - - - - -
_____

_____
- - - - - - - - - - - - - - - - -
_____

 Directions: Name each picture. Write *m* on the line if the word begins with /m/. Color the /m/ pictures.

 Home Activity: Have your child find pictures that begin with /m/ and paste the pictures on paper to make an /m/ book.

Name _____

✏️ Write 🖍️ Color

Mm

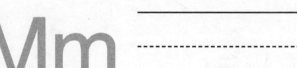

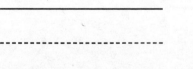

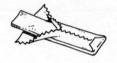

🍎 **Directions:** Name each picture. Write *m* on the line if the word ends with /m/. Color the /m/ pictures.

School + Home **Home Activity:** Have your child find an object at home that ends with /m/.

Name _____

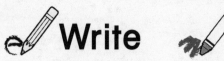 **Write**    **Color**

Tt

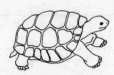

 Directions: Name each picture. Write *t* on the line if the word begins with /t/. Color the /t/ pictures.

 Home Activity: Have your child trace the target letter and name the pictures that begin with *Tt*.

75

 **Write**    **Color**

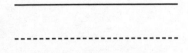

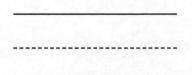

Tt

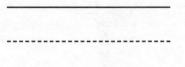

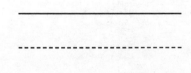

🍎 **Directions:** Name each picture. Write *t* on the line if the word ends with /t/. Color the /t/ pictures.

🏠 School + Home   **Home Activity:** Have your child draw a picture of something that ends with /t/ and write the word.

Name _____

 **Write**    **Color**

Color   Write

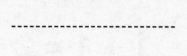

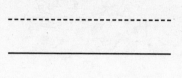

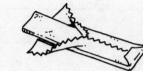

Aa

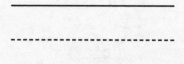

 Directions: Name each picture. Write *a* on the line if the word begins with /a/. Color the /a/ pictures.

 Home Activity: Have your child find other words that begin with /a/.

Name _____

 Write 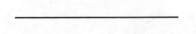 Color

_____
- - - - - - - - - - - - - - - -
_____

_____
- - - - - - - - - - - - - - - -
_____
- - - - - - - - - - - - - - - -
_____

$1 + 1 = 2$

Aa

_____
- - - - - - - - - - - - - - - -
_____

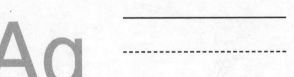

_____
- - - - - - - - - - - - - - - -
_____

_____
- - - - - - - - - - - - - - - -
_____

 Directions: Name each picture. Write *a* on the line if the word begins with /a/. Color the pictures with middle /a/.

School + Home **Home Activity:** Have your child find an object at home that begins with *a*, draw a picture of it, and write the word.

Name _____

 **Write**    **Color**

_____
- - - - - - - - - - - - - - -
_____

_____
- - - - - - - - - - - - - - -
_____

_____
- - - - - - - - - - - - - - -
_____

Ss

_____
- - - - - - - - - - - - - - -
_____

_____
- - - - - - - - - - - - - - -
_____

_____
- - - - - - - - - - - - - - -
_____

 Directions: Name each picture. Write *s* on the line if the word begins with /s/. Color the /s/ pictures.

 Home Activity: Have your child find pictures that begin with /s/ and paste the pictures on paper to make a /s/ book.

Name _____

 Write   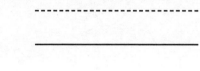 Color

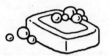

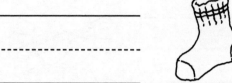

Ss

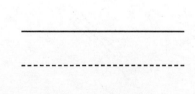

 Directions: Name each picture. Write *s* if the word ends with /s/. Color the picture if the word begins with /s/.

 Home Activity: Have your child find an object that begins with the letter *s*, draw a picture of it, and write the word.

Name _____

 Write    Color

_____

- - - - - - - - - - - - - - - -

_____

_____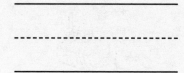

- - - - - - - - - - - - - - - -

_____

_____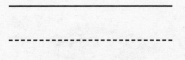

- - - - - - - - - - - - - - - -

_____

 **Pp**

_____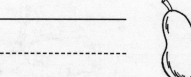

- - - - - - - - - - - - - - - -

_____

_____

_____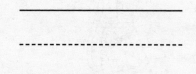

- - - - - - - - - - - - - - - -

_____

 Directions: Name each picture. Write *p* on the line if the word begins with /p/. Color the /p/ pictures.

 Home Activity: Have your child find pictures that begin with /p/ and paste the pictures on paper to make a /p/ book.

Name _____

  **Write** **Color**

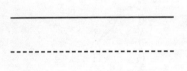

Pp

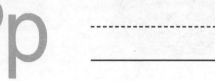

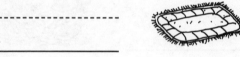

Directions: Name the pictures. Write *p* on the line if the word ends with /p/. Color the final /p/ words.

School + Home **Home Activity:** Have your child use the final /p/ words in sentences.

 **Write**    **Color**

Cc

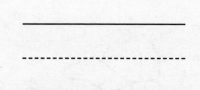

 Directions: Name each picture. Write *c* on the line if the word begins with /k/. Color the /k/ pictures.

 Home Activity: Have your child find an object at home that begins with /k/, draw a picture of it, and write the word.

Name _____

 **Write**  **Color**

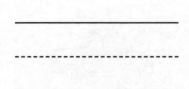

Cc

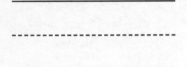

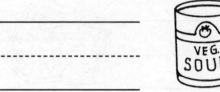

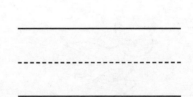

 Directions: Name each picture. Write *c* on the line if the word begins with /k/. Color the /k/ pictures.

 Home Activity: Have your child find other words that begin with /k/.

84

Name _____

 **Write**   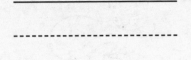 **Color**

_____
- - - - - - - - - - - - - - - - - - -
_____

_____
- - - - - - - - - - - - - - - - - - -
_____

Ii

_____
- - - - - - - - - - - - - - - - - - -
_____

_____
- - - - - - - - - - - - - - - - - - -
_____

_____
- - - - - - - - - - - - - - - - - - -
_____

 Directions: Name each picture. Write *i* on the line if the word begins with /i/. Color the /i/ words.

 School + Home **Home Activity:** Look through a newspaper or book with your child and point out words that begin with *Ii*.

Name _____

 Write    Color

_____
- - - - - - - - - - - - - - - - - -
_____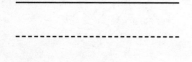

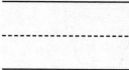 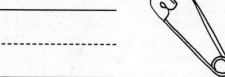

_____
- - - - - - - - - - - - - - - - - -
_____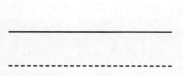

Ii

_____
- - - - - - - - - - - - - - - - - -
_____

_____
- - - - - - - - - - - - - - - - - -
_____

Directions: Name each picture. Write *i* on the line if the word has /i/ in the middle. Color the /i/ words.

School + Home   **Home Activity:** Help your child make a list of words with /i/.

Name _____

 Write    Color

_____
p ___ n

_____
m ___ p

_____
s ___ p

_____
c ___ t

_____
s ___ t

_____
p ___ n

 Directions: Write *i* or *a* to finish each word. Color the /i/ pictures.

 Home Activity: Have your child write *tip* and *tap* and draw a picture for each word.

Name _____

 **Write**    **Color**

_____
- - - - - - - - - - - - - - - - - - -
_____

_____
- - - - - - - - - - - - - - - - - - -
_____

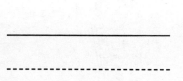 

_____
- - - - - - - - - - - - - - - - - - -
_____

 Ii

_____
- - - - - - - - - - - - - - - - - - -
_____

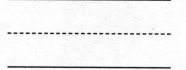 

_____
- - - - - - - - - - - - - - - - - - -
_____

_____
- - - - - - - - - - - - - - - - - - -
_____

Directions Name the pictures. Write *i* on the line if the word has /i/ in the middle. Color the /i/ pictures.

88

School + Home **Home Activity** Have your child draw a picture of something with /i/.

Name _____

 **Write**  **Color**

_____

- - - - - - - - - - - - - - - - -

_____

_____

- - - - - - - - - - - - - - - - -

_____

 Nn

_____

- - - - - - - - - - - - - - - - -

_____

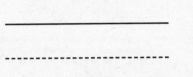

_____

- - - - - - - - - - - - - - - - -

_____

_____

- - - - - - - - - - - - - - - - -

_____

 Directions: Name each picture. Write *n* on the line if the word begins with /n/. Color the /n/ pictures.

 Home Activity: Have your child name other words that begin with /n/.

Copyright © Savvas Learning Company LLC. All Rights Reserved.

89

Name _____

 Write    Color

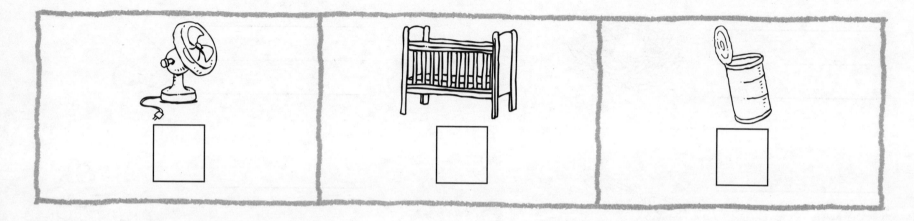

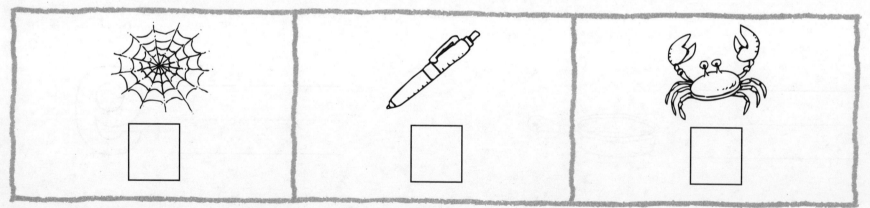

 Directions: Name each picture. Write the letter for the final sound in the box. Color final /n/ words green and final /b/ words blue.

 Home Activity: Have your child trace *n* and *b* and name the pictures.

90

Name _____

 Write   Color

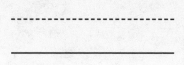 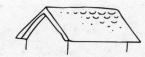

Rr

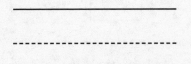 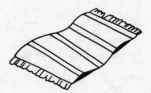

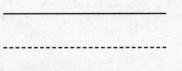 

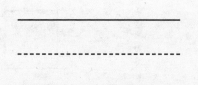 

 Directions: Name each picture. Write *r* on the line if the word begins with /r/. Color the /r/ pictures.

 Home Activity: Have your child find pictures that begin with /r/ and paste the pictures on paper to make an /r/ book.

91

Name _____

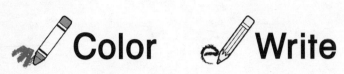 Color  Write

Directions: Color each picture that begins with /r/.
Write *r* in the box.

 School + Home **Home Activity:** Have your child name the pictures that begin with /r/.

Name _____

 Write    **Color**

_____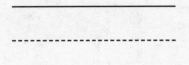
- - - - - - - - - - - - - - -
_____

_____
- - - - - - - - - - - - - - -
_____

_____
- - - - - - - - - - - - - - -
_____

Dd

_____
- - - - - - - - - - - - - - -
_____

_____
- - - - - - - - - - - - - - -
_____

_____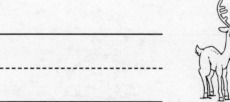
- - - - - - - - - - - - - - -
_____

 Directions: Name each picture. Write *d* on the line if the word begins with /d/. Color the /d/ pictures.

 Home Activity: Have your child find pictures that begin with /d/ and paste the pictures on paper to make a /d/ book.

Name _____

 Write    Color

_____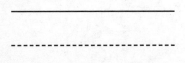
- - - - - - - - - - - - - -
_____

_____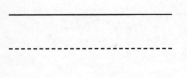
- - - - - - - - - - - - - -
_____

Kk
Dd

 (door)

_____
- - - - - - - - - - - - - -
_____

_____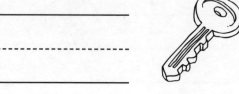
- - - - - - - - - - - - - -
_____

_____
- - - - - - - - - - - - - -
_____

_____
- - - - - - - - - - - - - -
_____

 Directions: Name each picture. Write *k* on the line if the word begins with /k/ and *d* if it begins with /d/. Color the pictures.

 School + Home **Home Activity:** Have your child find other words that begin with /k/ or /d/.

94

Name ________________________________

Write Color

Ff

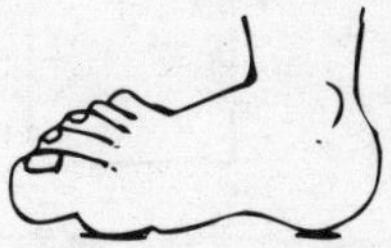

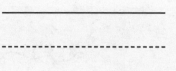

Directions: Name each picture. Write *f* on the line if the word begins with /f/. Color the /f/ pictures.

School + Home

Home Activity: Have your child find pictures that begin with /f/ and paste the pictures on paper to make a /f/ book.

Name _____

 **Color**  **Write**

Directions: Name the pictures. Color each picture that begins with /f/. Write *f* in the box.

School + Home **Home Activity:** Have your child name the pictures that begin with /f/.

Name _____

 **Write** **Color**

Oo

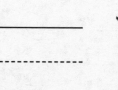

 Directions: Name each picture. Write *o* on the line if the word begins with /o/. Color the /o/ pictures.

School + Home **Home Activity:** Look through a newspaper or book with your child and point out words that begin with /o/.

Name _____

 **Write**   **Color**

_____
- - - - - - - - - - - -
_____

_____
- - - - - - - - - - - -
_____

Oo

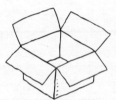

_____
- - - - - - - - - - - -
_____

_____
- - - - - - - - - - - -
_____

_____
- - - - - - - - - - - -
_____

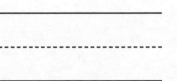

_____
- - - - - - - - - - - -
_____

_____
- - - - - - - - - - - -
_____

Directions: Name each picture. Write *o* on the line if the word has /o/ in the middle. Color the /o/ pictures.

School + Home **Home Activity:** Help your child make a list of words with /o/.

98

Name _____

 Write  Color

f x

m p

t p

Oo

b b

c p

b x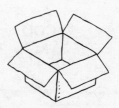

 Directions: Write *o, a,* or *i* to finish each word. Color the /o/ pictures.

 Home Activity: Have your child write *mop* and *map* and draw a picture for each word.

99

Name _____

 **Circle**  **Color**

fix fox		map mop	
cab cob		tap top	

Directions: Circle the word that names the picture.
Color the /o/ pictures.

School + Home **Home Activity:** Have your child draw a picture of an /o/ word.

Name _____

 **Write**    **Color**

_____

- - - - - - - - - - - - -

_____

_____

_____

- - - - - - - - - - - - -

_____

Hh

_____

_____

- - - - - - - - - - - - -

_____

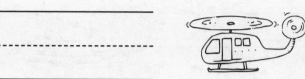

_____

_____

- - - - - - - - - - - - -

_____

_____

_____

- - - - - - - - - - - - -

_____

 Directions: Name the pictures. Write *h* on the line if the word begins with /h/. Color the /h/ pictures.

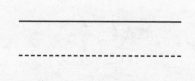 **Home Activity:** Have your child find other words with /h/ such as *hat*.

Name _____

 Write  Color

_____
- - - - - - - - - - - - - - - - -
_____

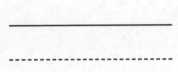

_____
- - - - - - - - - - - - - - - - -
_____

Hh

_____
- - - - - - - - - - - - - - - - -
_____

_____
- - - - - - - - - - - - - - - - -
_____

_____
- - - - - - - - - - - - - - - - -
_____

_____
- - - - - - - - - - - - - - - - -
_____

_____
- - - - - - - - - - - - - - - - -
_____

Directions: Name each picture. Write the letter for the beginning sound. Color the /h/ pictures.

Home Activity: Have your child write rhyming /h/ words for the words *cat, top,* and *sit* and then draw a picture for each word.

Write **Color**

_____
- - - - - - - - - - - -
_____

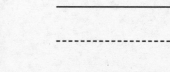

_____
- - - - - - - - - - - -
_____

LI

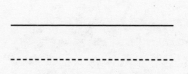

_____
- - - - - - - - - - - -
_____

_____
- - - - - - - - - - - -
_____

_____
- - - - - - - - - - - -
_____

Directions: Name each picture. Write *l* on the line if the word begins with /l/. Color the /l/ pictures.

School + Home

Home Activity: Have your child find pictures that begin with /l/ and paste the pictures on paper to make a /l/ book.

103

Name _____

 Write　 Color

 id

 mi

 hi

L l

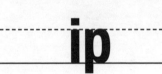 ip

 ap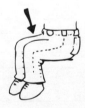

 fi

 Directions: Write *l* if the word begins with /l/. Write *ll* if the word ends with /l/. Color the pictures.

104

 Home Activity: Have your child draw a picture of something that begins with /l/.

Name _____

 Write 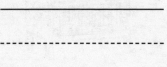 Color

_____
- - - - - - - - - - - - -
_____

_____
- - - - - - - - - - - - -
_____

_____
- - - - - - - - - - - - -
_____

_____
- - - - - - - - - - - - -
_____

_____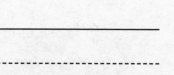
- - - - - - - - - - - - -
_____

_____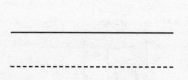
- - - - - - - - - - - - -
_____

 Directions: Name each picture. Write the blend for the beginning sound. Color the pictures.

School + Home **Home Activity:** Have your child point out initial consonant blends in the words in a book or magazine.

Name _____

 Write    Color

_____

ba

_____

ne

_____

mi

_____

ib

_____

ill

_____

ed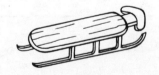

 Directions: Write the letters for the consonant blends to finish each word. Color the pictures.

 **Home Activity:** Have your child use the words in sentences.

Name _____

 Write    Color

_____
- - - - - - - - - - - - -
_____

Gg

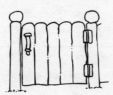

_____
- - - - - - - - - - - - -
_____

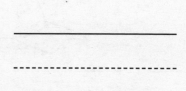

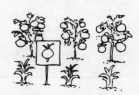

_____
- - - - - - - - - - - - -
_____

 Directions: Name each picture. Write *g* on the line if the word begins with /g/. Color the /g/ pictures.

 Home Activity: Have your child find pictures that begin with /g/ and paste the pictures on paper to make a /g/ book.

Name _____

 Write 　 Color

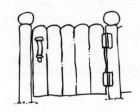

oat 　 do 　 be 　 ate

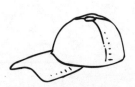

le 　 ap 　 um 　 pi

 Directions: Write the letter to finish each word. Color
the pictures that begin or end with /g/.

 Home Activity: Have your child name the pictures
that begin with /g/.

Name _____

 **Write**  **Color**

_____
- - - - - - - - - - - - - - - -
_____

_____
- - - - - - - - - - - - - - - -
_____

 Ee

_____
- - - - - - - - - - - - - - - -
_____

_____
- - - - - - - - - - - - - - - -
_____

_____
- - - - - - - - - - - - - - - -
_____
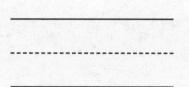

_____
- - - - - - - - - - - - - - - -
_____

 Directions: Name each picture. Write *e* on the line if the word begins with /e/. Color the /e/ pictures.

 Home Activity: Look through a newspaper or book with your child and point out words that begin with /e/.

Name _____

 Write    Color

---
- - - - - - - - -

- - - - - - - - -

Ee

- - - - - - - - -

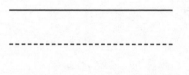

- - - - - - - - -

- - - - - - - - -

- - - - - - - - -

 Directions: Name each picture. Write the letter for the middle sound of each picture. Color the /e/ pictures.

 Home Activity: Help your child make a list of words with /e/.

Name _____

 Write  Color

h   n   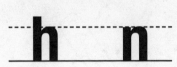

m   p   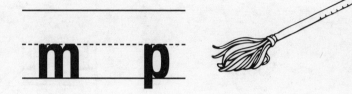

b   d   

Ee

p   n   

h   t   

n   t   

 Directions: Write *e, a,* or *o* to finish each word. Color the /e/ pictures.

 Home Activity: Have your child write *pen* and *pan* and draw a picture for each word.

Name _____

 Circle  Color

bed bad		bet bat	
log leg		pen pan	

Directions: Circle the word that names the picture.
Color the /e/ pictures.

School + Home **Home Activity:** Have your child draw a picture of
something with /e/.

Name _____

 Write    Color

_____
- - - - - - - - - - - - -
_____

_____
- - - - - - - - - - - - -
_____

Jj
Ww

_____
- - - - - - - - - - - - -
_____

_____
- - - - - - - - - - - - -
_____

_____
- - - - - - - - - - - - -
_____

_____
- - - - - - - - - - - - -
_____

 Directions: Name each picture. Write *j* if the word begins with /j/. Write *w* if the word begins with /w/. Color the /j/ pictures.

 Home Activity: Have your child find other words with /j/ or /w/.

Name _____

 **Write**    **Color**

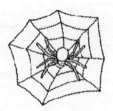

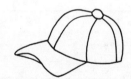

Jj
Ww

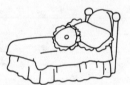

 Directions: Name each picture and spell the picture name. Write the word on the lines. Then color the /j/ and /w/ pictures.

 Home Activity: Have your child draw pictures of things that begin with /j/ and /w/.

114

Name _____

 Write   Color

_____

_____

- - - - - - - - - - - - - - - - - -

_____

_____   Xx   _____

- - - - - - - - - - - - - - - - - -   - - - - - - - - - - - - - - - - - -

_____   _____

_____      _____

- - - - - - - - - - - - - - - - - -   - - - - - - - - - - - - - - - - - -

_____   _____

 Directions: Name each picture. Write *x* on the line if the word ends with /ks/. Color the /ks/ pictures.

School + Home **Home Activity:** Help your child find pictures or words that end with /ks/ to make a /ks/ booklet.

Name _____

 **Write**    **Color**

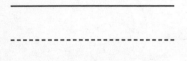

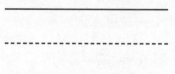

6

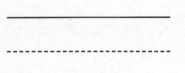

Xx

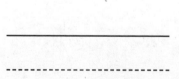

 Directions: Name each picture and spell the picture name. Write the word on the lines. Then color the pictures that end with /ks/.

 Home Activity: Have your child draw a picture of something that ends with /ks/.

Name _____

 Write    Color

_____

- - - - - - - - - - - - - -

_____

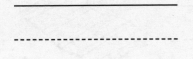

_____

- - - - - - - - - - - - - -

_____

Uu

_____

- - - - - - - - - - - - - -

_____

_____

- - - - - - - - - - - - - -

_____

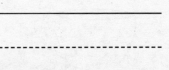

_____

- - - - - - - - - - - - - -

_____

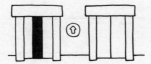

_____

- - - - - - - - - - - - - -

_____

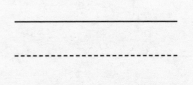

 Directions: Name each picture. Write *u* on the line if the word begins with /u/. Color the /u/ pictures.

School + Home **Home Activity:** Look through a newspaper or book with your child and point out words that begin with /u/.

117

Write   Color

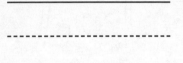 

  Uu

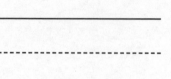 

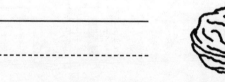

Directions: Name each picture and spell the picture name. Write the word on the lines. Then color the /u/ pictures.

 School + Home   **Home Activity:** Help your child make a list of words with /u/.

118

Name _____

 Write    Color

c   t      b   s

t   b      **Uu**   p   n

t   p      n   t

 Directions: Write *i*, *o*, or *u* to finish each word. Color the /u/ pictures.

 Home Activity: Have your child write *rug* and *bug* and draw a picture for each word.

119

Name _____

 Write  Color

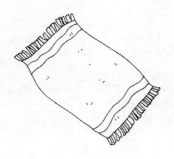

_____

- -

_____

_____

- -

_____

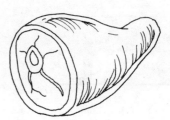

_____

- -

_____

_____

- -

_____

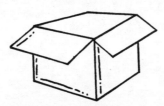

_____

- -

_____

_____

- -

_____

Directions: Say the word that names the picture. Spell the picture name. Write the word on the lines. Color the /u/ pictures.

School + Home **Home Activity:** Have your child draw a picture of something with /u/.

Name _____

 **Write**  **Color**

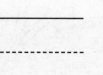 Vv

Zz

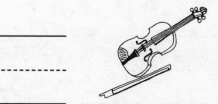

 Directions: Name each picture. Write *v* if the word begins with /v/. Write *z* if the word begins with /z/. Color the /v/ pictures.

 School + Home **Home Activity:** Have your child find other words that begin with /v/ or /z/.

Name _____

 Write    Color

_____
- - - - - - - - - - - - - - -
_____

_____
- - - - - - - - - - - - - - -
_____

_____
- - - - - - - - - - - - - - -
_____

Vv
Zz

_____
- - - - - - - - - - - - - - -
_____
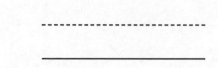

_____
- - - - - - - - - - - - - - -
_____

_____
- - - - - - - - - - - - - - -
_____
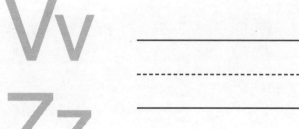

 Directions: Name each picture and spell the picture name. Write the word on the lines. Then color the /z/ and /v/ pictures.

 Home Activity: Have your child draw pictures of things that begin with /v/ and /z/.

Name _____

 Write  **Color**

_____

- - - - - - - - - - - -

_____

_____

- - - - - - - - - - - -

_____

_____

- - - - - - - - - - - -

_____

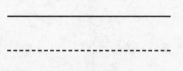 

Yy
Qq

_____

- - - - - - - - - - - -

_____

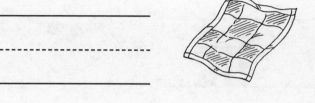

_____

- - - - - - - - - - - -

_____

_____

- - - - - - - - - - - -

_____

 Directions: Name each picture. Write *y* if the word begins with /y/. Write *qu* if the word begins with /kw/. Color the /kw/ pictures.

 Home Activity: Have your child find other words with /y/ or /kw/.

123

Name _____

 Write  Color

_____ilt

_____arn

_____ack

Yy
Qq

_____ak

_____ick

_____ell

 Directions: Name each picture. Write *y* if the word begins with /y/. Write *qu* if the word begins with /kw/. Color the /y/ pictures.

 Home Activity: Have your child draw pictures of things that begin with /y/ and /kw/.

124

Name _____

 **Write**    **Color**

m __ t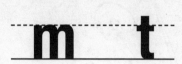

Aa
Ii

p __ n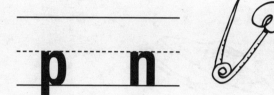

c __ b

k __ t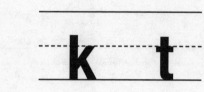

p __ g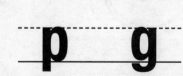

j __ m

 Directions: Name each picture. Write *a* or *i* to finish each word. Color the /a/ pictures.

 Home Activity: Have your child write *tin* and *tan* and draw a picture for each word.

125

 **Write**  **Color**

_____

- - - - - - - - - - - - - - - - -

_____

- - - - - - - - - - - - - - - - -

_____

- - - - - - - - - - - - - - - - -

_____

- - - - - - - - - - - - - - - - -

_____

_____

- - - - - - - - - - - - - - - - -

_____

_____

- - - - - - - - - - - - - - - - -

_____

 Directions: Say the word that names the picture. Spell the picture name. Write the word on the lines. Color the /i/ pictures.

 Home Activity: Have your child draw a picture of something with /i/. Then help him or her spell and write the picture name.

Name _____

 Write    Color

l **g**

m p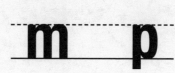

A a
I i
O o

t p

s ck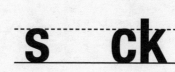

h ll

p t

 Directions: Write *a*, *i*, or *o* to finish each word. Color the /o/ pictures.

 Home Activity: Have your child write *lock* and *rock* and draw a picture for each word.

✏️ Write 🖍️ Color

![top]	![cap]	![banana/corn]
_____ - - - - - - - - - - - - - _____	_____ - - - - - - - - - - - - - _____	_____ - - - - - - - - - - - - - _____
![box]		
_____ - - - - - - - - - - - - - _____	_____ - - - - - - - - - - - - - _____	_____ - - - - - - - - - - - - - _____

Directions: Say the word that names the picture. Spell the picture name. Write the word on the lines. Color the /o/ pictures.

School + Home

Home Activity: Have your child draw a picture of something with /o/. Then help him or her spell and write the picture name.

Name _____

 Write    Color

_____
w   b

_____
l   g

_____
p   n

Aa Ee Ii

_____
h   t

_____
m   n

_____
j   t

 Directions: Write *a, i,* or *e* for each word. Color the /e/ pictures.

 Home Activity: Have your child write *hen* and *pen* and draw a picture for each word.

129

Name _____

 **Write**  **Color**

_____
- - - - - - - - - - - - -
_____

_____
- - - - - - - - - - - - -
_____

_____
- - - - - - - - - - - - -
_____

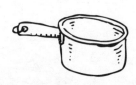

_____
- - - - - - - - - - - - -
_____

_____
- - - - - - - - - - - - -
_____

_____
- - - - - - - - - - - - -
_____

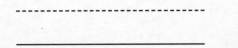 **Directions:** Say the word that names the picture. Spell the picture name. Write the word on the lines. Color the /e/ pictures.

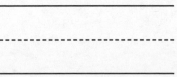 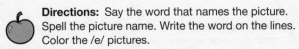 **Home Activity:** Have your child draw a picture of something with /e/. Then help him or her spell and write the picture name.

130

Name _____

 **Write**    **Color**

s ___ n

b ___ t

Aa
Oo
Uu

c ___ p

p ___ p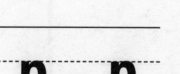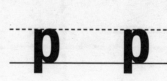

b ___ s

c ___ t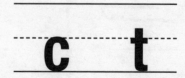

 Directions: Write *a*, *o*, or *u* to finish each word. Color the /u/ pictures.

 School + Home   **Home Activity:** Have your child write *hut* and *nut* and draw a picture for each word.

Name _____

 Write Color

_____
- - - - - - - - - - - - - - - - - - -
_____

_____
- - - - - - - - - - - - - - - - - - -
_____

_____
- - - - - - - - - - - - - - - - - - -
_____

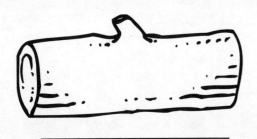

_____
- - - - - - - - - - - - - - - - - - -
_____

_____
- - - - - - - - - - - - - - - - - - -
_____

_____
- - - - - - - - - - - - - - - - - - -
_____

 Directions: Say the word that names the picture. Spell the picture name. Write the word on the lines. Color the /u/ pictures.

 Home Activity: Have your child draw a picture of something with /u/. Then help him or her spell and write the picture name.

Name _____

 Circle  Color

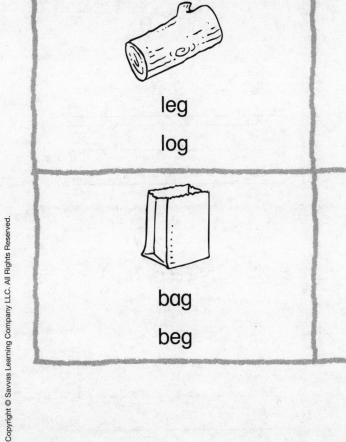

leg
log

pen
pan

pep
pup

bag
beg

led
lid

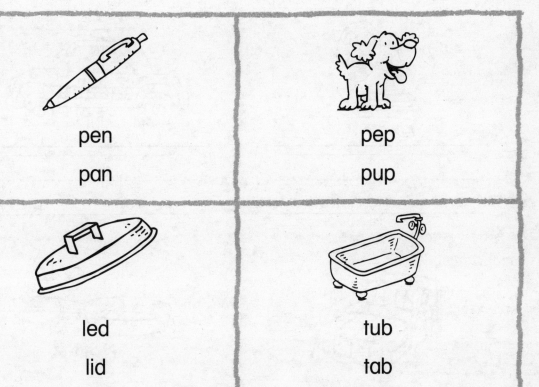

tub
tab

Directions: Circle the word that names the picture. Color the pictures.

School + Home
Home Activity: Have your child use the words in sentences.

Name _____

 Write  Color

_____

- - - - - - - - - - - - - - - - - - -

_____

_____

- - - - - - - - - - - - - - - - - - -

_____

_____

- - - - - - - - - - - - - - - - - - -

_____

_____

- - - - - - - - - - - - - - - - - - -

_____

_____

- - - - - - - - - - - - - - - - - - -

_____

_____

- - - - - - - - - - - - - - - - - - -

_____

Directions: Name each picture and spell the picture name. Write the word on the lines. Then color the pictures that rhyme.

School + Home **Home Activity:** Have your child use the picture names in sentences.

Name _____

 **Draw**

pin		cub		hut	
pen		cab		hat	
pan		cob		hit	

 Directions: Draw lines to match the words with the pictures.

 School + Home **Home Activity:** Have your child draw pictures for these words: *cat, cot, cut*.

Name _____

✏️ Write

_____
- - - - - - - - - - - -
_____

_____
- - - - - - - - - - - -
_____

_____
- - - - - - - - - - - -
_____

_____
- - - - - - - - - - - -
_____

_____
- - - - - - - - - - - -
_____

_____
- - - - - - - - - - - -
_____

_____
- - - - - - - - - - - -
_____

_____
- - - - - - - - - - - -
_____

🍎 **Directions:** Name each picture and spell the picture name. Write the word on the lines.

School + Home **Home Activity:** Have your child write *mop* and *map* and draw a picture for each word.

Name _____

 Write  Color

I	am

_____

_____ am a pig.

_____

I _____ a cat.

 Directions: Read each sentence. Write the missing word to finish the sentence. Color the picture.

School + Home **Home Activity:** Have your child use *I* and *am* in other sentences.

Name _____

 **Write** **Color**

| I | am |

_____

- -

I _____ a duck.

_____

_____

am a sheep.

_____

- -

_____ am a frog.

_____

- -

I _____ a goat.

Directions: Read each sentence. Write the missing word to finish the sentence. Color the picture.

 Home Activity: Have your child use *I* and *am* in other sentences.

Name _____

 Write    Color

(the   little)

_____
- -
The girl is _____.

_____
- -
_____ cat is little.

_____
- -
_____ dog is little.

_____
- -
The pig is _____.

🍎 **Directions:** Read each sentence. Write the missing word to finish the sentence. Color the picture.

School + Home **Home Activity:** Have your child use *the* and *little* in other sentences.

Name _____

 **Write**   **Color**

the   little

_____

_____ dog can sleep.

_____

I have a _____ dog.

_____

Did you feed _____ dog?

_____

The _____ dog sleeps.

Directions: Read each sentence. Write the missing word to finish the sentence. Color the picture.

 School + Home **Home Activity:** Have your child use *the* and *little* in other sentences.

Name _____

 **Write**    **Color**

| to | a |

_____

- -

Tim has _____ map.

_____

- -

Tim went _____ school.

_____

- -

Pam went _____ school.

_____

- -

Pam has _____ top.

Directions: Read each sentence. Write the missing word to finish the sentence. Color the picture.

 School + Home **Home Activity:** Have your child use the high-frequency words in other sentences.

Name _____

 Write ✏️ Color

```
┌─────────────────────────────────────┐
│    to      a     little     am       │
└─────────────────────────────────────┘
```

_____

- -

I am _____ cat.

_____

- -

I go _____ school.

_____

- -

I _____ a little cat.

_____

- -

The house is _____.

🍎 **Directions:** Read each sentence. Write the missing word to finish the sentence. Color the picture.

 Home Activity: Have your child use the high-frequency words in other sentences.

Name _____

 Write  Color

| have | is | little | am |

_____

- -

Flowers _____ petals.

_____

- -

The flower is _____.

_____

- -

I _____ looking.

_____

- -

The girl _____ looking.

 Directions: Read each sentence. Write the missing word to finish the sentence. Color the picture.

 Home Activity: Have your child use the high-frequency words in other sentences.

143

Name _____

 Write ✏️ Color

[have   is]

_____
- -
I _____ to go to school.

_____
- -
This _____ the school.

_____
- -
I _____ to go home.

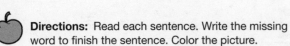

_____
- -
This _____ home.

🍎 **Directions:** Read each sentence. Write the missing word to finish the sentence. Color the picture.

School + Home **Home Activity:** Have your child use *have* and *is* in other sentences.

Name _____

 Write  Color

| we | my | like |

_____

- -

We _____ the cat.

_____

- -

We _____ my dog.

_____

- -

_____ like to tap.

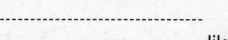

_____

- -

_____ pig is little.

Directions: Read each sentence. Write the missing word to finish the sentence. Color the picture.

School + Home **Home Activity:** Have your child use *we*, *my*, and *like* in other sentences.

145

Name _____

 **Write** **Color**

we	my	like

_____

It is _____ cat.

_____

_____ have a cat.

_____

We _____ the cat.

_____

We like _____ cat.

Directions: Read each sentence. Write the missing word to finish the sentence. Color the picture.

Home Activity: Have your child use *we*, *my*, and *like* in other sentences.

146

Name _____

 **Write** **Color**

| he | for |

_____

_____ has a pan.

_____

_____ likes the pan.

_____

The pan is _____ you.

_____

It is _____ Pam.

 **Directions:** Read each sentence. Write the missing word to finish the sentence. Color the picture.

School + Home **Home Activity:** Have your child write the words *he* and *for* using a fun material (yarn, sticks, glitter).

Name _____

 Write  Color

| for | he |

_____
- -
It is _____ Tim.

_____
- -
_____ can bat.

_____
- -
_____ has a bat.

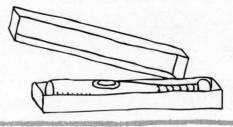

_____
- -
It is _____ Tim.

Directions: Read each sentence. Write the missing word to finish the sentence. Color the picture.

Home Activity: Have your child use *for* and *he* in other sentences.

Name _____

 Write  Color

| she | with | me | we |

_____

- -

Pam ran _____ me.

_____

- -

_____ like to run.

_____

- -

_____ ran to the mat.

_____

- -

Run with _____ .

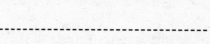 **Directions:** Read each sentence. Write the missing word to finish the sentence. Color the picture.

School + Home **Home Activity:** Have your child use *me, with, she,* and *we* in other sentences.

149

Name _____

 Write　　 Color

| she | with | me | little |

_____

_____ can jump rope.

_____

She can run _____ me.

_____

She can hop with _____.

_____

This is a _____ duck.

 Directions: Read each sentence. Write the missing word to finish the sentence. Color the picture.

 Home Activity: Have your child use *she, with, little,* and *me* in other sentences.

Name _____

 Write  Color

see   look

_____
- -
I can _____ the cat.

_____
- -
_____ at me!

_____
- -
I _____ for my cat.

_____
- -
Pat can _____ the dog.

 Directions: Read each sentence. Write the missing word to finish the sentence. Color the picture..

 Home Activity: Have your child use *see* and *look* in other sentences.

151

Name _____

 Write  Color

see	look	with	for

_____

- -

I can _____ the bird.

_____

- -

I can _____ for it.

_____

- -

It is _____ the cat.

_____

- -

Mom can run _____ me.

 Directions: Read each sentence. Write the missing word to finish the sentence. Color the picture.

 Home Activity: Have your child use the high-frequency words in other sentences.

152

Name _____

 **Write**  **Color**

| they | of | you | she |

_____

Can _____ see you?

_____

Can _____ see the top?

_____

It is a lot _____ fun.

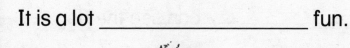

_____

_____ can see the fox.

🍎 **Directions:** Read each sentence. Write the missing word to finish the sentence. Color the picture.

School + Home **Home Activity:** Have your child use the high-frequency words in other sentences.

153

Name _____

 Write    Color

┌─────────────────────────────┐
│ they   of   you   we   │
└─────────────────────────────┘

_____

_____ can see the dog.

_____

They can run to _____ .

_____

I see a lot _____ dogs.

_____

_____ ran to me.

 Directions: Read each sentence . Write the missing word to finish the sentence. Color the picture.

School + Home **Home Activity:** Have your child use the high-frequency words in other sentences.

154

Name _____

 **Write**  **Color**

[are   that   do]

_____
- -
_____ they little?

_____
- -
_____ you like cats?

_____
- -
We _____ little.

_____
- -
_____ is a little hat.

Directions: Write the missing word to finish each sentence. Color the pictures.

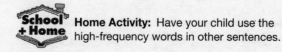 **Home Activity:** Have your child use the high-frequency words in other sentences.

Name _____

 Write ✏️ Color

| do | that | are |

_____

- -

_____ you see the man?

_____

Is _____ the lid?

_____

- -

We _____ at the top.

_____

- -

_____ you like my cat?

🍎 **Directions:** Read each sentence. Write the missing word to finish the sentence. Color the picture.

School + Home **Home Activity:** Have your child use the high-frequency words in other sentences.

Name _____

 **Write**  **Color**

| one two three four five |

_____

I see _____ flags.

I see _____ frogs.

_____

I see _____ rats.

I see _____ clips.

 Directions: Read each sentence. Write the missing word to finish the sentence. Color the picture .

 Home Activity: Have your child use *one*, *two*, *three*, *four*, and *five* in other sentences.

Name _____

 Write  Color

| one | two | three | four | five |

_____
- -

I can see _____.

_____
- -

I can see _____.

_____
- -

I can see _____.

_____
- -

I can see _____.

 Directions: Read each sentence. Write the missing word to finish the sentence. Color the picture.

School + Home **Home Activity:** Have your child use the number words in sentences to tell about things in your home.

Name _____

 **Write**  **Color**

here   go   from

_____
- -

Go _____ here to here.

_____
- -

We can _____ fast.

_____
- - - - - - - - - - - - - - - - - - -

You can go _____ .

_____
- - - - - - - - - - - - - - - - - - -

It is _____ me.

🍎 **Directions:** Read each sentence. Write the missing
word to finish the sentence. Color the picture.

School + Home   **Home Activity:** Have your child use the
high-frequency words in other sentences.

159

Name _____

 **Write** **Color**

here   go   from

_____

- -

Did you _____ here?

_____

- -

I did not go _____.

_____

- -

I had to go _____ here to here.

_____

- -

I will _____ here.

Directions: Read each sentence. Write the missing word to finish the sentence. Color the picture.

 School + Home **Home Activity:** Have your child use the high-frequency words in other sentences.

160

Name _____

 **Write**  **Color**

| yellow   blue   green   have |

_____

- -

The pond is _____ .

_____

- -

Is the sun _____ ?

_____

- -

My top is _____ .

_____

- -

I _____ a cat.

Directions: Read each sentence. Write the missing word to finish the sentence and color the picture.

School + Home **Home Activity:** Have your child use the high-frequency words in other sentences.

Copyright © Savvas Learning Company LLC. All Rights Reserved.

Name _____

 Write ✏️ Color

green   blue   yellow   for

_____
- -
My dog is _____.

_____
- -
I have a cat _____ you.

_____
- -
The hill is _____.

_____
- -
I like that _____ hat.

 Directions: Read each sentence. Write the missing word to finish the sentence. Color the picture.

School + Home **Home Activity:** Have your child use the high-frequency words in other sentences.

Name _____

 Write  Color

| what | was | said | she |

_____
- -
_____ she with you?

_____
- -
_____ is my mom.

_____
- -
He _____ she was with me.

_____
- -
_____ did you see?

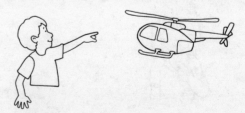
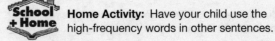

Directions: Read each sentence. Write the missing word to finish the sentence. Color the picture.

School + Home **Home Activity:** Have your child use the high-frequency words in other sentences.

Name _____

 Write   Color

| what   am   said   was |

_____
- -
I _____ five.

_____
- -
_____ can I do?

_____
- -
I _____ four.

_____
- -
I _____ I can help.

Directions: Read each sentence. Write the missing word to finish the sentence. Color the picture.

 School + Home   **Home Activity:** Have your child use the high-frequency words in other sentences.

Name _____

 Write  Color

| where | is | come | me |

_____

- -

Do they see _____?

_____

- -

_____ did you go?

_____

- -

_____ here, little dog.

_____

- -

My mom _____ here.

Directions: Read each sentence. Write the missing word to finish the sentence. Color the picture.

School + Home **Home Activity:** Have your child use the high-frequency words in other sentences.

Name _____

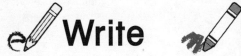 Write  Color

| come | we | where | she |

_____

- -

_____ can see me.

_____

- -

_____ will you go?

_____

- -

_____ can run fast.

_____

- -

_____ and see this bug.

Directions: Read each sentence. Write the missing word to finish the sentence. Color the picture.

School + Home **Home Activity:** Have your child use the high-frequency words in other sentences.

Name _____

 Write  Color

what	with	do	little

_____

_____ you like to jump?

_____

My dog is _____ .

_____

I will go _____ you.

_____

_____ can I do to help?

Directions: Write the missing word to finish each sentence. Color the pictures.

School + Home **Home Activity:** Have your child use the high-frequency words in other sentences.

Name _____

 Write  Color

| where | go | that | come |

_____

I will _____ with you.

_____

I can _____ with you.

_____

Did you see _____ ?

_____

_____ do you live?

 Directions: Read each sentence. Write the missing word to finish the sentence. Color the picture.

School + Home **Home Activity:** Have your child use *where, go, that,* and *come* in other sentences.

Name _____

 **Write**  **Color**

was	like	the	from

_____

- -

This is _____ big pet.

_____

- -

I _____ to run fast.

_____

- -

The box is _____ him.

_____

- -

I _____ the best one for the job.

Directions: Read each sentence. Write the missing word to finish the sentence. Color the picture.

School + Home **Home Activity:** Have your child use *was, like, the* and *from* in other sentences.

Name _____

 **Write**    **Color**

of	my	yellow	we

_____

This is _____ big pet.

_____

_____ like to jump.

_____

The sun is _____.

_____

Here are two _____ my hats.

🍎 **Directions:** Write the missing word to finish each sentence. Color the pictures.

🏠 School + Home   **Home Activity:** Have your child use the high-frequency words in other sentences.

Name _____

 Write    Color

| blue   they   have   four |

_____

Do I still look _____?

_____

We can _____ fun.

_____

The bed is _____.

_____

_____ play with a ball.

Directions: Read each sentence. Write the missing word to finish the sentence. Color the picture.

School + Home **Home Activity:** Have your child use the high-frequency words in other sentences.

Name _____

 Write ✏️ Color

┌─────────────────────────────────────┐
│ three   said   look   you   │
└─────────────────────────────────────┘

_____

- - - - - - - - - - - - - - - - - -

_____ at that bug.

_____

- - - - - - - - - - - - - - - - - -

I _____ I will run fast.

_____

- - - - - - - - - - - - - - - - - -

Do _____ like hot dogs?

_____

- - - - - - - - - - - - - - - - - -

I have _____ cats.

🍎 **Directions:** Read each sentence. Write the missing word to finish the sentence. Color the picture.

School + Home **Home Activity:** Have your child use the high-frequency words in other sentences.